Lessons of Darkness

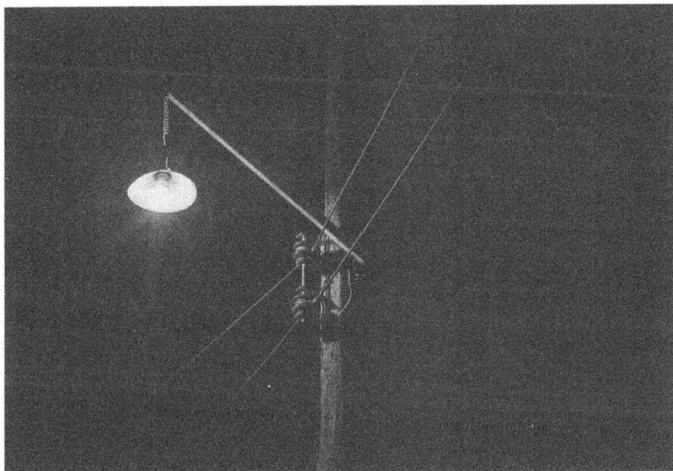

Poems by Alan Catlin

LUCHADOR PRESS

Luchador Press
Big Tuna, TX

Copyright © Alan Catlin, 2019
First Edition1 3 5 7 9 10 8 6 4 2
ISBN: 978-1-950380-69-5
LCCN: 2019954167

Design, edits and layout: El Dopa
Author photo: Valerie Catlin

Acknowledgments:

The author would like to thank the editors of these publications where some of the poems in this collection oriinally appeared:

"Dead Calm" in *Trajectory*, "Blue Angel" in *Big Hammer*, "True Romance," "Big Hammer," "A Bridge Too Far" in *Up the River*, "Cape Rock," "Reflections in a Golden Eye" and "Sixteen Candles" in *Chiron Review*, "Dead Reckoning," "Clockwork Orange" and "The Best Years of Our Lives" in *HPN*, "21 Grams" in *New Verse News*, "Mulholland Drive" in *Lummox*, "Black and White Night" in *Rye Whiskey Review*, "The Ugly American," "Branded to Kill" and "Lost Highway" in *Outlaw Poetry*, "Live and let Die" and "Dead Man" in *Asylum Floor*

TABLE OF CONTENTS

Jesus' Son

Before the Devil Knows You're Dead

Lessons of Darkness

Jesus' Son

Jesus' Son

There was something strange about him,
as if he'd been coming through the valley
of death on a white horse, the sun in
ascendance in one eye, and a glint of light
on a sword blade in the other, coming and
going with no particular destination in mind.
He had one of those cult worshiper badges
that identified him as a member in good
standing in some sub-rosa, white supremacy
organization that was so far underground
half of the members were moles.
Part of his street prophet mission was to give
inspirational readings from seminal texts
like *Decline of the West*, seemingly chosen at
random, after a bad night huffing airplane
model glue and chugging Tall Boy malt liquors.
Looked like one of those back lot imitation
revolutionaries from a Godard flick shot
in a junk yard in Flushing. A flick that ends
with an massive explosion that was supposed
to signify the end of consumer society
as we knew it, like the one staged by Antonioni
in Zabriski Point. But the whole enterprise
came off as just so much bad acting with the
cheapest props ever. Was so transparent even primary
school kids called him a phony, taunted him
by calling him Gluey to his face, a face that

had the distinction of being the only one
ever reproduced on a poster and sent to every toy
and hobby shop in the state with the warning:
Do Not Sell This Man Toy Model Products of Any Kind.
Proved the adage that: *a little learning is a dangerous
thing,* by considering the book *In the Belly of the Beast,*
as scripture and that the son of God, were he
alive today, would be packing heat and have shivs
concealed in the soles of his sandals. And if He
had a ride, man, he would drive it like he stole it.

The Night Has a Thousand Eyes

All she needed was a stage,
a high backed chair to perform
tricks on, an overhead spotlight
and a live mike and it was show time.
Was a self-styled Queen of Quirk,
part post modern projection
of all that could go wrong with
higher education with a concentration
in literary theory. Had a sense of style
that made even the most basic
wardrobe change an adventure,
a clash of mismatched items that
gave new meaning to eccentric.
Claimed to have a lover who could
make her come with a hand gesture
from afar. Dedicated her signature
performance piece, *Remote Control
Orgasm* to Rainier, her married lover.
Didn't have fans as such, but fanatics,
near cultish devotees, who would cut
themselves and offer to die for her,
on stage, if necessary, just to make
an impression. Her most ardent admirers
were the women with multiple suicide
attempts scars, black leather riding crops,
weight lifter muscles and elaborate
South Asian tattoos. All the others were
either neophytes or pretenders.

Played the German Bilding bad girl role
to the max despite having grown up
in Queens. She was going places.
All the way to the top. Now, all she needed
to do, was to die young.

The Killer Inside Me

We ask for no mercy. Expect none.
Cage fighting, forged in an alliance
of white power with crack whore
on a field of inbred genes, bad blood
rampant in cesspit leakage, brown field's
forever banners proudly unfurled.

We ask for no mercy.
Chokeholds, bare knuckle bashings,
round house, off balance, vital organ
leg kicks. Blood in the urine, sperm
fluids, anal discharges, just another day
in the gym, in the cage, ultimate fighting,
no time matches; only the winner
emerges alive.

What's an orbital socket among friends?
A spleen? A few extra teeth?
We ask for no mercy
Grant none. Earn modest purses for
the Cause, the Third Reich's and the Fourth.
Corner men with silks sewn in patterns
that reveal secret societal ties, HH
tattoos, the signifiers and the signified.

We ask for no mercy. Expect none.
Scars make your body more dignified,
make us your worst nightmares embodied,
bestow us with your blitzkrieg, your white
lightning rod iron on patches, your Death's
head rings, each one a poison pill holder
for such time as.....Losing is never an option.

We ask for no mercy.
We receive none. Live stream us on pay per
view cable TV events, Dystopia Now !
There's a widget for this.

Dead Calm

*No matter what anyone tell you, all addictions are
the same. You've got to keep upping the dose.*

-Reed Farrel Coleman

Five storyes up and you can feel
the heat rising from the street.
81 degrees at midnight, listening
to Mahler 9 on the crap radio,
listening to the work of a man
who knows he is about to die.
Fire escape slats hot iron rails,
leaking rust, melt rubber soles
on contact. Heat lighting illuminates
the low, clinging clouds beyond
the tight blocks of high rise
dumps. Every window open,
house lights dim, no relief from
the still, dead air.

The first cold drink tastes as
sour as the fetid night.
Slow drinking cheap beer from
ice packed stein does not assuage
a lingering thirst, makes drinking
a futile exercise of rote movements;
nothing accomplished, nothing
gained. Not enough money for
serious hard liquor, intoxicating
drinks. Five storeys down doesn't
feel like nearly enough.

Blue Angel

Alive is a relative word.
        -Philip Marlowe

After elite college education,
all honors everything, working
gofer jobs, barely affording
eighth floor walkup digs,
drug and casual pill popping
becoming a requiem for a dream
kind of existence she imagined
an improbable, happy ending for.
Used up, burned out at twenty-eight,
a refugee of numerous lockups,
psyche wards, one rehab stay from
left for dead in urban hell hole in
shooting gallery squat where even
the slime balls won't go.
Gainfully, Outreach referred, employed:
cleaning toilets, urinals, scrubbing
floors on hands and knees.
Life a post industrial, heavy metal rave,
a nightmare gone as bad as it gets.
Was it penance or punishment?
She asked herself in rare lucid moments
between all enveloping black hole
memory gaps, massive cognitive
dissonance, enhanced by massive
EST regimen. Was unrecognizable

in mirrors as the person she might
have been, or become, pushing sixty
inside and out, though admitting to
almost thirty years of age seemed like
the worst kind of sick joke.
Spent her days inhaling bleach fumes
and cleanser chemicals until her eyes
and throat bled. Started putting something
aside every payday for one last score
that would end it all.

Firestarter

That they survived the 60's, the 70's:
the politics, peace marches, riots,
demonstrations, multiple arrests,
assumed identities, underground
living, plots against the state, more
radical politics, experimental drug
taking, bomb tossing, all the predicate
felonious follies of youth-was a minor
miracle. Found themselves in some
backwoods nowhere, well on the way
to being someone else, a well-stocked
chemistry lab the only holdover from
former lives. He, a kind of idiot savant
with a periodic table and formulae;
worked overtime trying to create
the ultimate Huxley high: soma, the one
described at length in Utopian novel
Island. A drug that insured peace and
love and blissed out harmonic states,
one that would make him the ultimate
Dr. Feelgood, after all everyone had
their own connection in the 60's:
The Kennedy's, professional ballplayers,
soldiers on patrol in the field..... It was
what people did while the women worked.

He said, *Try this.*
She said, *What is it?*
Something like LSD.
How different?
Don't know. Let's try it and find out.

So they did.

Their genes didn't exactly explode
but they could feel their brains rewiring,
could feel their hair start to smolder as
if it might spontaneously combust.
Felt incredibly alive in ways that were
hard to define and not always good.

Sex was amazing on the drug.
Everything was amazing.
For awhile.
Under the influence.
Until the child was born.

An exceptional one in every way.
Who had powers that shouldn't be
allowed but once they were unleashed...

A little child shall lead them.

Women's Prison

To the destructive element submit yourself
                -Joseph Conrad

Work for her was finding new
and better ways to screw the poor,
the innocent, and the oppressed.
Was descended from a long line
of malefactors, demagogues, sadists,
and straw boss men and women:
border guards along the California
state line denying on-the-run-from
Dust Bowl hell Okies, Palmer no-
knock, no warrant, home invaders,
tower guards with instructions to
shoot to kill all Japanese internees
on the run, professional strike breakers,
Pinkerton club wielders, head busters,
riot inciters, dirty tricksters one and all.
As jail matron she ascended through
the ranks by crushing the wills of the prisoners.
Became expert in enhanced interrogation
techniques, a skill set that transitioned
well into the private Jail Industrial
Complex. Drew the blackest of lines
in her ledgers and maintained the margins
of profit come hell and insurrection.
Loved that her word was law and that
there were no recourse, no appeals,

no mercy shown. All the inmates feared
her almost as much as the boot lickers
and ass kissers that worked the yard,
especially the ones chosen to be sex
slaves, subject to her whims and desires;
a situation she jokingly likened to a
perverted extreme rendition. Burning out
on the job under her acquired a new meaning
among the rank and vile. Sure it was lonely
at the top, she said, sipping fifteen year old
unblended whiskey, feet up and crossed
on her supersized desk where she signed
all the official and unofficial death warrants,
Draconian decrees, and anything else she
felt the need to proclaim. Yeah, it was lonely
to be totally in charge but it was a good feeling
to. Felt the way God must feel on a good day.

Separate Tables:

an elegy for the old guys

The oldest of them all, regulars
at the bar, never failing to invite
everyone present to his wake,
whenever that would be.
It will be a hell of a party.
Too bad I'll miss it.
And it was.

And his nearest crony always
claiming he was more interested in
his golf clubs than a wake,
no matter who's it was.
To which the oldest guy always
replied, *Over my dead body.*
He cried the hardest and the longest
of everyone not his wife.

And the dirty old man, cancer-
ridden-bald always insisting on
changing the channel from HLN
to women exercising,
I'll be dead soon, what do I need
more bad news for?
And he was right, he didn't.

And the house drunk, whose ignorance
was compounded daily by his insistence
that he was the world's authority
on everything, despite ample evidence
to the contrary. Who didn't have a
drinking problem more alcohol couldn't
cure. Three strokes later, in his early 50's,
going cold turkey against doctor's advice,
he finally proved stupidity, once and
for all, is its own reward.

And the day guy who slowly,
methodically, drank a case of beer
a day, working or not, famous for
the bad jokes he could never remember
the punch line to.

And The liberal and the bigot,
each pretending the other did not
exist, in the same bar, ordering the
same food, the same drinks, every
day for years.

All of them gone now.

No one takes their place.

We Were Warriors

What did he expect?
Leaving his off-the-lot,
totally loaded sports coupe
running, sound system blaring
Killah Rap, outside inconvenient
store where he, either was delivering
or purchasing, by appointment only,
new shipment of stuff. *K-12 for
the masses,* could have been the slogan
on his custom made silk screen top,
but even he, as capo of this less than
wonderful chain of storefronts in
highly undesirable locations, must
have realized that kind of advertising
was a dead giveaway for the actual line
of work he was engaged in.

Discovering his vehicle AWOL was
a source of considerable angst given it
was a not reportable as stolen, cash-only-
purchase soon to be found up-close and
personal with immovable object, totaled
beyond all recognition, out of gas, and
stripped of anything of value, including
product, in even more undesirable location/

slum, in territory marked as belonging to
rival business associates, in formerly
equally turfed out city. It was enough
to make a priest fornicate with whores,
he said, led to a declaration,
This means war.

And it did.

They are still counting the bodies.

Dazed and Confused

They are leaning against The Van,
a vehicle that might have passed
state inspection once, but not in anyone's
recent memory. Stand staring in direction
of free range kids: the boys with home-
styled Mohawks, gang banging someone
else's kids, holding him down and whaling,
until the blood flows. The girl's looking
like a cross between Raggedy Anne's worst-
hair-day-nightmare, and a street walker in training.
Will bad mouth anyone who refuses their
request for cigarettes, though they are
years away from double figures in time
spent upon this earth.

Mom speed balling thin, chain smoking
no-brand, no-tax Mentholated death butts,
eyes perpetually glazed in kiln fires
by amateur artists, nipple piercings tearing
through soiled tank tops, bare midriff exposed
to better reveal, infected rings, demented
cell block tattoos of mutant butterflies in flight.

The man is chug a lugging PBR's from cans,
shoulder length hair unwashed for weeks,
faded, sleeves-removed T says, *Charlie Daniels
Band*. Mother Trucker arm tattoos over swastikas

and White Power logos, his face looking as if
he had been used as a workout bag for a heavyweight
fighter, or, worse, by a biker gang stiffed in a drug deal.

The free rangers are raising holy hell
in the playground, manning the monkey bars,
commandeering the slides, the swings,
pummeling all who stand in their way,
a veritable force of nature until the Man
runs out of beer and bellows,

*Get your asses over here, like now, or, I'll cut
you a new one.* And they move, as if electrically
charged, as if they have known worse things
to happen, and could imagine whatever that was,
happening again.

The Tenth Victim

Their idea of a fun in the sun
was an off-the-grid retreat
involving kidnapping, grand theft
auto and miscellaneous felonious
assaults, all taking place well after
the multiple keg tapping, homemade
wine tasting and white lightning in
a jar.

Once everyone was assembled,
face painting began using wild roots
and found berries, colors inspired by
commando models like John Rambo
look alikes remaking themselves as
dead ringers for the cast of the
Lord of the Flies. Take your pick which
version.

Blood sacrifices were common, following
pig roasts, while the coals were still
hot, metal spits still in place greased
and ready for the eighth, ninth and tenth
victims of the night. Victims were gathered
by stealth patrols, along unmarked paths,
lakeside retreats, fishing shacks and

hunting lodge habitats. No one suspects
a thing until it is too late.

Each year they choose a new
location. So far not even old bones
have been found.

True Romance

*What doesn't kill you leaves you feeling broken
and insane.* -Laura van den Berg

Theirs was a relationship of ecstasy
nights and train wreck days.
Roller balling in traffic against the lights
in a kind of cosmic chicken game
where there were no winners, just broken
bones and concussion protocols.
Ignored brown death cigarette pictures,
on black heart warning packets,
they extracted unfiltered off-brands from.
Used their street connections, ultra-mobile
maneuverability expertise, to run product
into places no one else would go.
Worked for guys who wore black bowling
shirts with someone else's name sewn on
the pockets. Who smoked El Ropo Parodi
brand butts that exuded a kind of toxic cloud
so thick even the slick lanes beyond seemed
like a bad dream apparition.
Thought their lives would be determined
by a major score, one where they were dealing
hot product from a battered suitcase they
would store in a classic car lifted from a lot
with security cameras so sharp they could
determine all their bona fides down to

the cup size of her padded bra.
Saw themselves heading due South,
top down, radio cranked to mega loud
country rock, a jungle full of monkeys
on their back.

A Bridge Too Far

The Douglas McArthur days
were the best of his life, outlining
battle plans on maps, in day rooms,
no one else could see. Used broken
chess pieces to mark troop placements
for advancing armies against battalions
so well entrenched, they might as
well be invisible.

Finally, more or less socialized,
his manner in Group, ranged from
aloof to hostile. Was often openly
aggressive, claiming he had more
important issues to attend to than
discussing non-essential problems
with civilians. The others were openly
rebellious, acting out as opposing
forces would when confronted
by an enemy.

Daily medication adjusted,
he became so passive as to be
effectively inert. Sat in far
corners of every communal room,
eyeing chess boards where headless
kings, defiled queens, disfigured knights,
lay on the defaced field of battle;
so many pieces missing, there was
never enough for a game.

Ride the Pink Horse

Dried blood in sawdusted ring amid the hoof prints
      and the uncaged cat's impressions.
The notches in the wooden spin the Wheel of Fate
      where thrown knives struck close to a female
      person of interest.
Discarded costumes on caravan beds and high backed
      chairs; table top ash trays full and overflowing.
Tipped over liter bottles of whiskey and wine completely
      drained and dry.
The carbon stained blades of the swords used for swallowing
      fire and tempered steel.
High wires and trapeze swings, hanging limp and off-balance
      between bent tent poles and ripped canvas peaks.
The chipped black anointed strong man's weights bleeding
      rust onto padded mats.
Rows of animal cages where the wild ones paced; the scent
      of their dried dung lingers.
Cracked funhouse mirrors: the concave and the convex ones,
      reflecting infinite distorted worlds.
Shooting gallery rifles disarmed: bent needles nearby, broken
      bottles, crushed smoke blackened cans.
Spider webbing spun on cotton candy cones.
Inert, weighted try your luck toss 'ems.
Stalled merry go round; chipped and cracked, beheaded ride 'ems.

Peeled poster people in three rings of fire.
Clown cars lined up for a funereal parade.
Squirt in the face flowers.
Confetti shooting guns.
Midway screams.

White Mischief

The look they were trying to
cultivate was pure early MTV
Billy Idol video: twin bleached
blonde, pointy locks razor cut
on one side to the nubs. They might
not totally look like out-of-a-bottle
platinum if the light was right, but
on the whole, were fooling no one.

Days not spent on the street pushing
penny ante grifts were used for
strong arming pensioners for their
wallets and their bags. He must
have spent days in public bathrooms
in front of badly tarnished mirrors
perfecting his snarls and his sneers,
while she worked various low rent
trades: shoplifting designer duds or
turning fifteen dollar tricks. Her new
thing was practicing two finger pocket
picking saying, *Everyone should
have a skill and a trade.* Said that
straight-faced as if she meant what
she did was some kind of gainful
self-employment.

On a whim, loaded on top shelf tequila
and some quality Hawaiian weed,
they decided on a white wedding day.
Broke a display window in a major
highway Salvation Army store and lifted
a second-hand dress and shiny at the knees
and elbows, tux. *A second hand gown*
is just right for a second hand woman,
but I ain't paying no $50 for a dress
I'm only going to wear once.

Hopped into his high rider, went pedal
to the metal singing, "Dancing with
Myself" as they skidded West off
the highway and into the trees:
no air bag impact absorbers. No seat belts.
Some people take them out.
Ain't easy neither.
Don't know why.

Men with Guns

Every night is a heavyweight
championship fight in low down,
Gomorrah among the evergreens, bar.
This roadhouse, this badass juke joint,
sleazebags flocked to, drawn as if
by some kind of base homing instinct
like poison river salmon to spawn.
All the men, side armed and switch
bladed, red eye hungry for poontang
and sour mash, one primal scream
away from shackled to a floor in
a rubber room. Don't bother calling
the heat as they wouldn't come this
far beyond cell tower service, even
if they got the call. All the barkeeps
are strapped tight with nickel plates,
have sawed-offs under the wood,
next to lead weighted batons, saps
and pepper sprays. Karate belts are
of no use here except for binding
hands and feet before, during and
after beatings. Disputes are settled by
blunt force trauma, internal organ
bruising and bloodletting; what passes
for sport this side of civilization.
All the roadies for the rock a' billy
bands are armed guards, semi-automatic,

hair triggered, madmen, like all the people
who hung out at the bar. More than once,
the end time, all night parties, looked
like the aftermath of a natural disaster,
localized cyclonic weather events;
complete ruination and smoking ruins.
Everyone chips into rebuild.
There is no place else to go.

Dead Heat on a Merry Go Round

Around town he was known as
the Mad Hatter. Always wore
a kind of straw boater thing that
hadn't been in style since the year one.
Carried a much opened and refolded
Daily Racing Form in his right rear
pants pocket, all his picks circled.
Had a stub of pencil behind each ear
handy for taking numbers, betting
slips, sports bets. If you could wager on
it, he'd get you a line. Even an exhibition
game. Did the rounds once a week
on lower Broadway collecting football
sheets, a drink in every bar, never once
wavering or stumbling out of the gate.
Amazed everyone how much such a skinny
old guy could pack away, how many pools
he had a piece of. His motto seemed to be
*A kickback in every saloon, watering hole
and backroom, after-hours card game.
Did you ever get busted?*
Hell no. Why would he? The heat were
among his best customers. Knew where they
could get a no-questions-asked cash loan.
With interest, of course. No special favors
offered, none expected either.

Paid cash and better than any track, state
sponsored lottery, sports book in and out
of town. On time. No questions asked,
no forms to fill out, no taxes.
Power ball?
What do I look like John D Fucking Rockefeller?

Had one armed bandits openly displayed
in bar tops around own, ten per cent of all
the jukeboxes. Need ciggies? Ask the Hatter,
he'd even supply the machine. At cost.
He was a one man, no body guards needed,
operation. No one in his right mind even
thought about rolling him. Nobody but new-
to-town-don't play-by-anyone's rules mob.

They made a mess out of that old man but
nothing like what was going to happen to them
when they got taken down. Maybe they thought
they could get away with murder but there were
long odds against that happening. The cops
made sure of that. And when they were caught,
it wasn't to downtown lockup they went but
to Hatter's associates, cruel men that made
cartel capos seem like Sunday school teachers,
the ones who specialized in the evil that men do.
Took they guys out of town for tractor drag
races where the robbers were the drag, shackled
by chains to hitches, bouncing over furrows,
flayed alive the slow way by dirt and rocks

and broken glass. Finally consigned to an immersion tank sort of alive: a fifty gallon drum filled with kerosene and set on fire. What was left was Davy Jonsed off the back of a commercial fishing boat at night well beyond the two mile limit.

Full Metal Jacket

Hard core!
            -Animal Mother

We were sick in The Green.
Was the only way to fly.
There were more gook ears, per
person, in our squad, than in any
other unit in the field. We were
so tuned into wasting slant eyes
we gave new meaning to the phrase:
'hard core motherfuckers.' And
proud of it.... There wasn't a single
conscience in the bunch. Anyone
had a soul they sold it to a Mama San
for a pipe of O and a boom boom
girl for a weekend beyond dreams.
Hell, even the green piss they passed
off as beer, tasted half decent after
a couple of pipes and the kind of
sex acts those girls were famous for.
They were some righteous pieces of tail...
We did down time the same way we
did our killing: 110 percent full out,
all the way....Sometimes, after a fire
fight, we'd string up some unlucky
bastard light a fire under his feet just
to watch them burn. A lot of money
changed hands betting on how long

before he talked. They all did in the end....
Sometimes we'd get a whole brace
of those black pajama Judas's , take them
up with airborne raiders, push a couple out
the gun ship bays and watch the last guy
pissing his pajamas. Scored some of our
best intel that way....Ever seen a dead man
smoke? One time we propped up a zeroed
out guy against a wall, stuck a lit butt in his
mouth, pulled his helmet low over his eyes
like he was collecting zzz's instead of nails,
and doesn't some dumbass pussy freelance
dude with a camera take a snap....went
international....'after a hard day in the field
a dead tired soldier takes a nap'...or some
such shit. You wonder how guy's like
that , those adrenaline junkies with a Nikon
survived? A lot of them didn't. Saw that
Flynn guy not long before he disappeared
in the Green. He was a cool dude , I'll give
him that. Not shy with a bowl or a babe.
I hate to think what those fuckers did to him
and his buddy. Well that's war for you.
Those were the days.

The Lobster

In the end everyone wears a blindfold; isn't that how
the story goes? "True Ash"

Every night at the Club Apocalypse Now!,
a Halloween party in hell, not so much dress up
as creatures escaped from the Island of Dr. Moreau,
clamoring for more. The front rooms are all
claustrophobic, the back rooms worse, like sealed
cells in a Poe story, the walls moving closer,
a hidden heat source intense as it gets, the air
inside, fetid with smoke machine clouds, so humid
the air drips blood. At midnight the barroom
morphs into a locked-in ward, a come-as-you-are
party after the inmates have raided the costume
racks mixing and matching period piece clothing,
rubber masks and fright wigs. Most of them look
like bodies freed from an open grave in a Stanley Spencer
charade, reel to reel tapes unleashing an assault of noise
like the soundtrack to Marat/Sade repurposed as
an ice capades theme show: the criminally insane
on ice. Towards morning the soul searching begins
a kind of scavenger hunt for the damned, body parts,
instead of hard boiled eggs and candy as the reward.
By dawn, they are all vampire white, refueling with
Red Bull, monkey dust and hydroponic pot,
high tension wired donning alternate reality goggles,
the kind that makes everything night vision glasses green.
Everyone is locked and loaded for a frontal assault.
A low chanting begins as they double time advance:
OSAMA MUST DIE OSAMA MUST DIE.....

Body Heat

Amazon was the name she used
when dancing. Not that she was
large or muscular or had a breast
removed. Quite the contrary.
If anything she was slim, had modest
firm breasts, *More than mouthful is
a waste,* she liked to say.

Wore a t-shirt that said, *Irony instead of
wrinkly.* Sprung for a tattoo on her
pubic bone that said, in Gothic lettering
with an arrow pointing down:
This way to paradise.

*I'll bet you made some tattoo artist
one happy dude.* Goons who came to
watch her perform said.
I had a babe do it, asshole, was her
standard reply though it was a lie.

The only breast surgery she ever
considered was: augmentation but
she eventually 86ed that idea:
stripping and sliding up and down a
pole was not a lifelong ambition.
Was waiting for Mr. Lucky, some
self-involved dirt bag with more money

than brains who thought with his dick
and could not conceive anyone could
take him, Mr. Mover and Shaker, down
a long forest path to the end. Once she
got her fangs in him, she'd be headed down
easy street, every cent, in every numbered
overseas bank account hers, and no one
would be able to take it back.
Someone had written a novel about her
and called it *Doom Fox*, but no one knew
this but her and the author, and he was
so far gone now no one remembered his name.

Liked to say, *Mama, didn't raise no*
Stepford Wives. Hell, no, in spades.
And she was living proof that was true.

Had a serial killer's face tattooed
on her left ass cheek with a legend
that said: *I laid Ted Bundy and lived.*
Is saving her right one for someone
extra special.

Hot Spot

A 92 in the shade and climbing, afternoon.
A one horse town with two options.
The married babe asks the new guy in town,
You have a TV? He says, *No.* looking her
straight in the eyes. *Well, that leaves you
only one option then. Good luck with that.*
She might have added a third possibility,
You drink? And he would say, *Not anymore.*
Meaning not any less either.

Tin can alley just-off-the-street, club, near
the flea bag no-tell motel with a no knock,
legs spread, whorehouse upstairs. In between
sets a blind drunk jazz pianist plays his own,
peculiar kind of blues on an out of tune piano,
in low lit, low life, no future night.
Even the horse flies have nowhere to go.

Is the kind of night a gun for hire killer shoots
the wrong man and wastes his main squeeze
just to see the blood flow, to watch dead girl
swirlies in the soon-to-be-clogged crapper.
A four fifths of a quart of Johnny Walker Blue
down and a fifth to go kind of night. Knows he's
next of the hit parade, once a screw up, always

a screw up. A dead one. This far down the throat
of the beast and another swallow to go. Feels the heat
from the blacktopped two lane, feels like it's
a sunrise in hell and there's nowhere else to go.

Lord of the Flies

All along Western Avenue, Washington,
down Central, to Broadway, he roams,
preaching the gospel of the New Church
of Latter Day Sinners. Quotes rock lyrics,
whole songs, albums even, as if they
were the living word of some divine being.
Tries to sell pamphlets, relics, stolen objects
from cemeteries: wreathes, flower sprays,
small veteran flags, whatever can be stolen
he appropriates as his own. Uses proceeds
to buy sweet brandies, pernod, fortified
wines; the higher he gets, the more vocal
he becomes. Tries every grift in the book
for a buck, enters church circles, wedding
receptions, prayer meetings, spontaneous
rugby scrums in bars, like some revenant
being left over from Coleridge or Keats.
Is never discouraged by rejection, insults,
anything short of an arrest, reinforced
with night sticks and plastic cuffs.

The orderlies at the drunk tank won't touch
him. *What would be the point?*
Once had a dog named Bingo but the health
department took him away. Put him down.

Said that animal had infections no one had
a name for yet. Still, the preacher was
impervious to disease like some kind of
uber menschen Elmer Gantry of the alcoholics;
might outlive Methuselah after surviving
record cold winters on the street, being hit,
in no particular order: by a Lyft driver,
a city bus and a garbage truck. No respectable
disease would go near him and he's had
all the other ones and lived. How do you
kill something like that? You don't.
Where he comes from death isn't the issue,
living is.

Before the Devil Knows You're Dead

The Big Sleep

Sirens splitting headache into
dream fragments. All part of some
urban war hell, door to door death
like Beirut in the 80's, like bombed
into oblivion Syrian cities, the Iraq oil
fields made for burning...

Ash clogged rain on cracked window
panes suggests it is only this badass
town burning down from the edges in,
to a soundtrack from some early black
and white Lynch movie where waking
is what dreams used to be once everyone
had fallen over the edge into nightmare...

Needles of light poke holes in the center
of unfocused eyes, blood stains never
painted walls, ceilings sag where broken
pipes leaked in that time before sleep
was invented. Women were portraits, then,
sketched by an artist gone mad, severed
ears hanging by loose filaments of skin;
even the white paint had impurities in it.
No one questioned what anyone had
to say then. Even the fires were less
frequent and the ash that fell was pleasing,
soothing, almost like snow on newly
mounded earth.

Grandmother

The old lady across the street watches
neighbors with late husband's field glasses
propped on a swiveling stand. Glasses so heavy
she can't hold them herself, but are as accurate
as an infantry field officer needed them to be
in the last great war. She is wizened, shrunken,
has eyes like that owl in Twin Peaks in the woods,
who is presumed to be observing everything.
Whose call in the night is meant to signify,
in a cliché cinematic way, something is about
to happen, or has happened, that will greatly
change major plot lines in the show or on
the street. This owl is not quite like the symbol
of spiritual significance for native peoples
as the poetry collection, *When the Owl Cries
Indians Die* does, suggestive of a journey
into other worlds, on scared grounds,
far removed from a small urban street divided
into blocks that are actually territories
for rival drug lords, meeting in the middle
to construct makeshift memorials for foot
soldiers killed in the line of duty.
She's seen it all, this forward point observer,
may not be the wise old granny of fairy
tales and myths, may not even by owl like
in her imparting of knowledge, but she sure
can deliver a witness identification profile,

and save authorities time, manpower, and effort
as the go-to-person for street crimes and
general on-the-hot-spot information.
On the street they added her to the time-honored
statements of Inevitability which now reads:
death, taxes and grandma.

Eyes of Laura Mars

Time was she had a name like:
Mary Jane, Donna Sue or Lu Anne.
Perused a hurricane list until
she found one that suited who
she imagined she might if
she were someone else.
Thought of herself as Camille,
with a Zero to Cat 4 personality:
high winds and a lot of moisture
where it mattered. Became someone
men would find exotic, would invent
cocktails in her honor, ones that would
knock you flat and take days to recover
from after. Following a session in bed,
she imagined the scars she had left
on her lover's back, the blood she
took and bathed in that came as if it
were from sacrificial lambs.
Closed the eye in her storm so
that no man would ever rest once
she caught him as prey and held on.
Sucked all the air out of any room
she did time in and rubbed skin
the wrong way, against the grain,
like sandpaper or a rasping file.

Once Camille had run her course
she shifted to a more plain,
but just as dangerous, Diane.
Became sultry as a no star tropic night
with death scents in a fetid, low tide
wind. The nearby beaches thick with
soft shell crabs fleeing the sea expending
light like radioactive waste. The sea can
no longer sustain the life that lies within.

Casablanca

Sweet dreams are made of these

Late night, low lights in the bar,
the only prop missing: a beautiful
woman in an evening gown and a tenor
sax for mood music. Must have been one
of those nights out of central casting;
swank hotels full, lounges shut down,
piano bars short a key man; nowhere
for a classic blonde, in a cut-to-the-thigh,
white dress to go, but here.
What can I do you out of? The bartender asked.
I need something warm inside me. She said.
You've come to the right place.
I certainly hope you're the man who can
give me what I need. What do you suggest?
Depends upon how warm you want to be
and how far inside you want to go.
Oh, all the way inside. And I want to feel hot.
You look like a Strawberry Blonde to me.
Even if I wasn't, I'll bet you could make me one.
All right if I smoke?
Certainly. It would be my pleasure to light you up.
I snapped the Zippo open and shut.
Put the red cocktail down before her on the bar.
You're a real fast worker. Anyone ever tell you that?
What else can you do?
Name your pleasure.
We're still talking about cocktails, aren't we?

Sure we are. Cocks and tails are my specialty.
A girl can never be too careful. You know,
I wouldn't want to be disappointed.
Don't worry, I rarely get complaints.
She smiled. Withdrew another cigarette from
a gold case. Tapped it on the bar and put one end
between parted lips. The barman didn't hesitate
to provide her light. It felt like the beginning of
a beautiful friendship.

Reflections in a Golden Eye

All the neglected women,
whose husbands don't care,
who spend their nights playing poker
with the boys or are on business trips
to places where after dinner cocktails
are extended to nightclub lounges
where bartenders accept tips in exchange
for clues to where the action really is:
at the strip clubs that offer fifty dollar
lap dances with all the back room trimmings
that can be written off on heavily redacted
expense accounts, no name vouchers,
services rendered left vague for an add
on fee.

All the neglected women,
for whom one man is never enough:
golf caddies, pool skimmers, tennis pros,
touring pros, swimming coach pros, racket ball
partners, pizza delivery guys. One long,
ugly vicious cycle, that leads to unintentional
suicide: prescription pills, don't- ever-
mix-drugs with designer cocktails.
Mourned by no one outside the service sector.

All the neglected women,
everywhere, at all times, throughout history and
now, wounded in places where scars
do not show, shopped-doctor medicated
for all occasions: bonded bourbon and unblended
whiskies, hip hip hooray everyday is a holiday
false cheer, sad demeanors poorly hidden behind
the best cosmetic surgery money can buy.

And the estranged children they never talk to.
Their wills are always contested.

Sixteen Candles

There they are: the wannabe Lolitas
on down escalators, these mega-mall
punkettes graduating from middle
school to juvenile detention centers,
these strip mall Goths, wearing too tight
short shorts with rainbow colored tights
beneath, walking barber poles with
neon eye shades, deep purple lip
gloss, dyed green hair in pig tails
acting like phony proof of age adult
film divas, Traci Lords tourists,
on the make, licking soft ice cream
on waffle cones, buzzed on big brother's
stash, drugs of unknown origin;
all they knew was a couple of puffs
and you were gone, way gone,
like mindless astronauts on earth,
weightless and floating. They exuded
a scent more powerful than mother's
back-of-the-bottom dresser drawer five
hundred dollars an ounce, special-occasion-
perfume, the kind of stuff male's of
the species sensed in their lizard brains
long before they encountered the bearer,
was more urgent, more alluring than

the video crack they were addicted to,
signaled a kind of slow motion rut in
progress or about to be. Who cared
if blood was spilled. If a separate,
unresolved crime followed after.

Dead Reckoning

The greatest enemy of man is alcohol.
But the Bible says to love your enemy.

                                        -Jack Taylor

Used to be men would wake up
in places like this, order a hair of
whatever dog that had been biting
them, and proceed with the business
of dying the slow death. Now they
just go on Facebook or Twitter in
the comfort of their own flophouses.

Still, some of the hardest of hard core
persist, inhaling the confined, dead
air of a down on its luck, well past its
prime, bar. The damp rancid beer,
residual smoke, wet rot in not-cleaned-
for- a-generation drains, the aggressive
slime, the mold, the fermented hops and
yeast, residuals as potent as advanced
narcosis of flesh, in active decay, suggesting
all these bodies lingering here may already
be dead while the mind is functioning
by rote, primary directives: heart beat,
breathe in/out, drink, pass out, wake up,
drink. One continual ellipse of unmodified
behavior. Everything on the cuff, dead
reckoning slated for the other side.

Eyes Wide Shut: a medley

Somewhere along the line, electrical
circuits in his head had become a study
in crossed wires. The scent of electrical
fires lingered on his breath, leaked
through open pores, leftovers from
some disaster porn show like a closed
room execution site he had been intimately
associated with. His eyes twitched,
muscles spasmed without visible reason,
some kind of uncanny Tourettes thing
that began after having been exposed,
at too an early an age, to multiple viewings
of *The Shining.* Remembered how it was
to be tyke on a bike, hot wheeling through
hedge mazes, up and down identical corridors
that never seemed to have a way out. Or maybe,
his afflictions could be traced to having
snuck into a Room 237 like place and seen
himself in a mirror, drawing blood images
of the future on the glass, knowing nothing
could change the bloody outcome to be
once you have been mired in what has past.
Saw himself as a voyeur, experiencing his
life through someone else's eyes. Knew
himself to be a Peeping Tom, prone to peering
through keyholes, raised shades, parted blinds,
spying on women he imagined were nude models

like Marilyn but were, in fact, body doubles for
Shelly Duvall. Imagined them stepping naked
from showers, rising up from hot baths, haloed
in ethereal mists, all the windows opaque,
the mirror, steam smudged over; his fingerprints
and those of myriad others who came after.
Their stripped bare bodies slick and glowing
with a film of rinse water and essence oils almost
within his grasp but not quite, smeared as they
were by Kubrick colors, Red Rum on the rocks.
All the eyes in the mirror, open wide, shut.

Shadowman

Even asleep, he dreams of being awake,
unable to sleep, sees himself on stage,
an audience of thousands at a black and
white movie of someone else's life watching
him as if he were both the subject and the object.
Senses his life is a series of perfect Kafka
moments: in both heaven and hell at the same
time with closed doors to chose from, each one
offering an escape to nowhere.
Then he seems himself in court, defending himself
before a Congress of Insomniacs, all of whom
are threatening to fall asleep. Feels as if his life
is being held together by strips of duct tape
and that his brain is trapped in some kind of
ongoing fugue state suffering a series of psychotic
reactions like mini-strokes, each one more
debilitating than the last. Hears the morning
room mirror crack as he shaves himself with
the honed edge of a clam shell, feeling Giacometti
thin and shrinking; just one more drunken
angel hitchhiking from Gospel to Gomorrah.

In a studio he records Martian music,
reads from scores dictated directly from God
whose presence is manifest in all the messages
scammed from street vendors and gravediggers.

Proudly claims to be directly descended from
a long line of Resurrection Men, *A dying
profession, even then*. Said, with a straight
face, and meaning it as the black sheep stricken
from the family tree with an axe and a bludgeon.
Makes do, with others of his kind, as a leader of
a team of disaster tourists, who make their living
pick pocketing dead people at mass casualty scenes.
Takes morning strolls, in his dreams, in minefields,
using prisoners of war as sweepers. Says he wants
to film the interior of his mind but all anyone would
see is shadow men painted on outdoor graffiti walls,
chalk outlines where the bodies had lain.

Somewhere in the Night

All the tables at the Hard Luck Café
have unbalanced legs and the all-weather
carpet has seen too many seasons,
so much spillage, no one knows what
color it might have been. Circulating
the air meant moving fetid remains
of poorly prepped for the Big Sleep bodies,
cadavers left in family crypts in exposed
coffins that developed aromas like spoiled
food left in walk-ins that lacked proper
coolant. The only people who could confuse
the Hard Luck with the Hard Rock Café,
were tripping their tits off college students
looking for high life after dark and an easy score.
All they found was a place so dank and
forbidding, light so low, even seeing eye
dogs could lose their way. In the gloom,
all the women looked as alluring as Grade B
movie stars, like the almost-made–it girls
looking for a role; all of them with the best
bodies, the best face lifts, money could buy.
The men were all midnight cowboys, in off
the rack suits, that would look better on
someone else, a few sizes smaller. Paid for
drinks with stolen credit cards, hoping against
all hope, one of them would not be declined.

On dim lit, solo acts only stage, strung out,
end of the line chanteuse sing in foreign
languages of endless nights, lost loves,
death in high heels and purses/shoulder
holsters, concealing serial numbers missing,
stolen guns. No one ever listens.

True Crimes

I was alive when I died. That's the problem.
-Richard Hambleton

In her prime, she could have
been Deborah Harry with a whiskey
voice looking like three packs of
cigarettes a day just this side of death.
Had the bearing and wardrobe of a Moroccan
rent boy gone to seed and was proud of it.
Quite an accomplishment for a women not
yet 30.

Was the kind of woman director's cast
as an ingénue but should have given her
whips and a leather suit and told her to
express her inner self. Took the uptown
express all the way to the end and found
one of those high rise death traps health
inspectors wouldn't get caught dead in
as a squat. Inside the flat was even worse
than could be imagined from the garbage
strewn, rat and roach infested, nightmare
in the hallways. Was so beyond seedy
anyone but the completely gone addict
would have second thoughts even stepping
inside.

What she called home was a crime scene
complete with forensic evidence and murder
books. Wore toe tags as a fashion statement,
she claimed, but really, it was all about saving
time and eliminating confusion. Who knows
who or what she would look like nine days gone?

After they wheeled her out on a gurney zipped
up tight, in a black rubber body bag, someone said
she was famous once but no one knew for what.

Night in the City

Smash and Grab is what they called
their act when they performed on
stage. The name was only partially
facetious. When they concluded their
act, the front man said, *I'm Smash*
and he's Grab. Men watch your wallets
on the way out and ladies, stay close
to your man. It got a laugh every time
though it shouldn't have.

In between gigs at rat hole, left-over-
from-the 60's cafes, cellar tea houses,
wine and cheese bars that smelled as if
something had been left to rot in the cellar,
of the street cats that made their home there,
getting fat and lazy feasting on rodents
and other lower forms of life, they performed,
up close and personal, in back alleys,
inside cheap, by-the-night, no-tell hotels.

Answered to a man named Louie,
who they owed large. A guy not to be
trifled with who was, on one hand a
walking mob boss cliché and, on the other,
the one who pulled all the strings in town despite
working out of a swap shop on Utica Avenue
in a place that was always one fire code violation

away from demolition, not that anyone dared
to issue the summons. The last guy who tried
was treated to a, no-expenses-paid vacation,
on a trauma ward with his jaw wired shut
and both arms broken so bad he might never
write again.

Smash and Grab might have been a decent
duo, might have been confused with Simon
and Garfunkel, if one of them could sing
and the other one could write. Grab, the taller
of the two had a Bill Medley haircut and semi-
soulful eyes, though any comparison between
the two ended there. Smash, was short and compact,
but not in a muscular way, more like a feral way,
that served him well, after nights at whatever club
they were playing to an audience of tweakers
and nodding hop heads, when they shook down
one of Louie's delinquent clients and the occasional
wet work. The ones who lived, bore the mark of
the man: his signature back of the hand burn
mark, administered with the hot end of
a Cuban cigar. A distinctive scar on two
hands meant you were a two time loser.
The third, on the forehead, meant you were dead.

Wag the Dog

Starting out he was a kind of
regional dee jay at a station whose
range could be measured in candle
power rather than in megawatts.
Spun tunes that ranged from pay-
by-the-hour studio recordings to
My Cheatin' Heart CxW standards.
Filled gaps between songs with corn
pone down home humor and banjo
picked tunes he stole from unknown
wannabees, whose best chance of reaching
Nashville, on their own merits, was
by hitchhiking the Interstate.
Married early and often: for a dirty
weekend, a month, one time, for almost
a year, never bothering with niceties like
annulments or divorce. Saw himself as
moving up and on from his humble
beginnings to another life where his
special traits: a toothsome smile, a lying line
of shit, and an amiable pat on the back
after an off-color joke, were considered
an asset on the job. The job of an elected
official. Having no moral compass
helped. Subscribed to the theories of the
immortal Satchel Paige who suggested:
never to look back because someone might
be gaining on you. Someone with a gun and
blood liable on his mind.

A Clockwork Orange

Maybe they thought what they did
for kicks exempted them from harm,
made them more than four bit, life
wasted, hoods that they were. While
young they were juvenile delinquents,
they were never children, they rolled
younger kids for lunch money. Moved
onto middle school mayhem as criminals-
in-training, selling reefer to 8 year olds,
on credit, charging interest that would
make a loan shark blush. By the time of
their first adult charges they were already
predicate felons skilled in the dark arts of street
crime. Saw themselves as moving
forward on a career path that would reap
larger rewards. Rolled street people and
busted wino skull with aluminum bats
because they liked the sound the bats made
when perfect contact was achieved.
Knew these implements would never break,
in the clutch, the way a wooden bat would.
Pissed on the remains after, because they could,
thinking of their victims, not as real people,
but a lower form of life. Stole pocketbooks
from old ladies in parking lots, pushing them
to the concrete to certain broken hips and limbs,
even after they made the score. The howls

they made on contact made them feel alive.
Even smiled for the security cameras as they
were booking to waiting cars. Thought, somehow,
if they drove fast enough, and far enough no
one could catch them. Liked to hit the same
places multiple times as if no one was paying
attention, as if every cop phone, lap top, message
board in five county radius didn't have their
faces on the top of their watch lists. Tried
ransacking neighborhoods, parked cars, unoccupied
homes, storefronts, like they were barbarian
hordes. Were one black and white car from an all-
hands-on-deck call that would put out
all the raging fires they harbored inside
with gasoline.

Shallow Grave

Each of us in our own private hell
      -Patrick Hoffman

Creating connections was easy when
you were young, handsome/beautiful,
easy to make on the club scene/circuit.
A deep soul kiss exchange in a crowd,
right hand sliding the goods into loose
fitting under garment, left hand palming
the cash payment in kind.

Expanding the business was more of
a tell-your-friends where you got
it, word of mouth. It's not like they
could advertise. As long as the goods
were quality, on time and hassle free,
everything was copacetic. No muss no fuss.
Staying under the radar of the cops
and the mob was what it was all about.
Everything was cool. Until someone OD'd.
Then it was everyone's business.
As in a whole new ball game.

The big players wanted their part of the action.
No was not an acceptable answer. Invited
the beautiful young ones to a screening
of a silent movie, a short subject, the muscle
had learned the content of doing tours
of duty in some heavy, no nonsense, places.

Showed a small shallow, oblong hole,
maybe three feet deep, at night in some
place that could only be described as
remote. As in Godforsaken.

Showed a man made immobile by duct
taping his limbs tightly together. Made mute
by sealing his mouth the same way. Only his
eyes bulging. His struggles to break free, futile.

Two masked men carry him to the hole.
throw him in and begin filling it in.
Who needs a sound track for that?
They made it clear there was one in case
someone might not be convinced
what they saw was real. It wasn't necessary.
The special effects spoke for themselves.

Business was brisk after that. Mistake free
and efficient. Not as profitable as before,
nor not nearly as much fun as in the old days.
What was?

21 Grams

Mountains are hard to climb
thus walls are your friends.
Learn your walls.

    -Bukowski

We laugh at your walls.
Drug cartel tunnel rats.
Digging from one safe house
to another safe house.
Under border fences, razor wire
enclaves, ICE patrol car roads.

We laugh at your walls.
Tunnels for shrink wrapped
pure. White death by the pound.
Powdered snow by the kilo.

We laugh at your walls.
Tunnels under prison walls.
Two and half miles of digging.
No problema. Cell to freedom
service. *Viva El Chapo!*
Viva Empire of the Opiates,
Reign of terror Take Two.

We laugh at your walls.
Steel stanchion impediments
where concrete is called for.

Easily breeched by purchased
at Wal-Mart, Home Depot,
Lowe's, metal cutting tool department.

We laugh at your walls.
Tunnels for coyote caravans,
pay the tolls, travel the underground
railway. *Refugees show us the green,
hombre and we deliver the goods.*

We laugh at your walls.
US Army supplied terror cells
of the night. Drug enforcers,
Zeta killers, Sinaloa lackeys,
CIA trained Torquemada's.

Slipping under barriers, walls.
Mescal high, take- no-prisoners
instructed, rape and pillage experts,
mercenaries for moola, hostile
and loathsome, heartless as
the street criminals they once were,
laughing at walls.

Find a tunnel and fill it, ten more
are dug. Once you are in The Life,
The Life is in you, there is no looking
back, no escape possible: one foot in
Sodom, the other in Gomorrah.
Not point in last wills and testaments:
no one will bury you when you are killed
unless the tunnel you are in collapses.

Before the Devil Knows You're Dead

Ghosts never die. Their windows are always lit.
        -Patrick Modiano

In the right light, she might have
passed for the kind of woman
she wanted to be. Thought years
would vanish if she wore a custom
designed slogan t-shirt that said:
Kurt Cobain Died for Our Sins,
under an unbuttoned, sheer white,
silk blouse. Wore form fitting leather
pants. Red high heels. All the most
expensive facial creams, highlighters,
wrinkle removers, known to man.
Wore glossy mauve lipstick and too
much matching eye shadow, in an attempt
to distract someone from all she would
prefer no one saw, as some kind of
cosmetic sleight of hand trick, in lights
turned down low, lounge. A dull,
incessant, heart beating, techno bass
line/ noise gradually increases as
witching hours approaches and passes,
as the hour between dog and wolf nears,
as shadow men and women gyrate in
something like a St. Vitus dance in overhead
flashing, post rave, highlights. All conversation
on eternal pause, frozen in mid-speech,

as barmen pour iridescent drinks into
tulip shaped flutes and the solo women at
the bar multiply; their acetylene eyes,
their benzene breath, as they press their
lips against glass leaving imprints in blood
wherever they touch, apply eye wash where
they sit, using an acid drip, bold and Teutonic
as Valkyries hitching a ride. Mouthing the words,
Got a light? to the only lovers left alive,
the await fire to be applied, drag deeply on
Camel shorts, in long thin ivory holders,
blowing perfect ovals into the dark, back room,
of just another sad café, all the tables empty
except for the ones three old men sit at, reciting
lines from Sartre plays: the ones the Nazis
didn't get, the ones the partisans did.

Kilo Two Bravo

but not it's the waiting on death.
it's not death that's the problem, it's the waiting.

        -Bukowski

My Daddy was a tunnel rat.
He used to say, hunkered down in
a forward operation base bunker,
drinking no label beer as flat as it
was warm, in some desert outback,
seven klicks from hell. *Once you've*
crawled down a hole into the belly of
the enemy's beast, there's no coming
back. Shit does something to you.

Maybe whatever the shit did to his
daddy was transferred to the genes,
was a post traumatic stress reaction
that went soul deep. Whatever it was,
the experience did not translate into a
How to Parent Your Impressionable Child
model text. Might be found in a DSM
but not in your standard Dr. Spock.

Made him more than a little crazy in
the field, after enlistment, which was an
asset in a fire fight but not in an existential
crisis that required clear thinking and sound

judgment. A high kill ratio earned you some street creds and a couple of stripes but when it came to tactical thinking; not so much.

Not that anyone could train for what
they had to deal with: trapped in a minefield,
on recon, the point man down and bleeding
out from missing limbs, three comrades to-
the-rescue, shortly thereafter, also down or
shell shocked; one sucking chest wound
and a missing limb from just another DOA
in a body bag.

And the rest of the patrol paralyzed,
afraid to move, not sure whether to proceed
with rescue attempts, to back track, or pray
for diving guidance, realizing this place
was not so much a grid of human devised
traps, but a random scatter of gully washed
death. What now, they thought? The dead
and the dying, the frozen and the terrified,
all of them awaiting orders. But who would
give them?

The Best Years of Our Lives

Their parents must have been flower children.
The kind of New Age hippies who renounced
all worldly goods, embraced the earth and created
a commune from found objects: discarded furniture,
broken appliances, and dead fall.
Shared everything equally: husbands and wives.
Especially the wives. Despite all the rhetoric
otherwise, peace, love and harmony, the husbands
always ruled.

The women had sunflower tattoos on
their backs, roses on their ankles, hearts and
flowers on their inner thighs. And the men had
peace symbols embossed on tops of their
feet. Wisely, all could be hidden by straight life
clothes, thinking that, in the short run, they might
have to take temporary jobs in the world.
Never considered the temp work would
become permanent careers in stock broking
and bond trading, accounting and high finance.
Totally selling out the life styles they had
valued above all else until the harsh winter,
short food supplies, lack of indoor plumbing,
made back to the earth just another nice sounding,
drug infused, high ideal. None of them looked back
from where they were now with fondness, pretending
youthful indiscretions were best forgotten despite

indelible reminders otherwise. More than one
long weekend, on the road accounts executive,
was amazed to find under straight-laced, hard driving
ice queen's stern demeanor, hid a wild woman whose
knowledge of the carnal arts rivaled those of women
found on South East Asian sex tours.

None of the Trustafarian, wasted youths, suspected
their parents had been anything other than what they
seemed despite odd body art they had devised a
cover story for. Not that their perpetually stoned,
less than zero, children cared one way or the other,
about potential wild times, high crimes and misdemeanors,
in their mamas and their papas summers of love.
As long as their plastic problem remained solved,
life was good. Who cared about sordid truths,
potential inherited biological time bombs,
their questionable parentage? None one really knew
where they came from, right?

Fire Walk With Me

After yet another night of serious
drinking, after last call at the bars,
the stumbling drunks to their cars.
After the bumper car rides around
campus circle, the tag-your-it fender
benders, the mad rush to the ultimate
greasy spoon diner, the eatery out
of some grade B black and white noir,
maybe the one used in *The Killing,*
Detour, The Postman Always Rings
Twice... After the spinouts onto
muddy, back lot, campus fields,
mellowing the beer and tequila shot
high with bong hits and pick me-up-pills.
After, literally, falling out of no-designated-
driver needed cars into deep, frozen rutted
parking spaces, ascending short stairs,
opening once-a-month-broken-glass door,
into no-joy-in-this-life waitress stations,
along the Formica topped counters and
once plush booths. After ordering eggs
over easy and keep-those-hash-browns
coming sides. After the never prepared for
inevitable weekends that start on Thursdays
rush, short order cook, drip sweats onto
cleaned-once-a-year-whether-it- needs-it-or-
not griddle. Then, someone push buttons

remote jukebox song selections, picking
a tune no one wants to hear, the one that
makes everyone's ears bleed, as if all here
inside was trapped inside some David Lynch
Twin Peaks sequel, where a seam in time
has been breached and all the evil others
are spilling into this life, devouring bodies
and souls like Egyptian Gods of the Dead,
exacting judgment on the unsuspecting.
And after the first song ends.
As the smoke from a dozen lit cigarettes
mixes with the burning griddle grease near
the nicotine and bacon fat stained ceiling,
the flip side of the song no one wanted to
hear, drops onto the turntable and a diamond
point needle slides into the groove but there
is no one left to listen.

The Serpent's Egg

He was the kind of reverse Midas drunk
that everything he touched either broke or died.
Was a kind of science experiment in aberrant
behavior, among hell's lower echelons, existing
among the drug abusers, sex perverts, money grubbing
pimps and whores, all of them two steps into the
grave and sliding away. Never thought about all
the corpses that turned up after he'd been somewhere,
as if he were the Johnny Appleseed of Death,
staggering about in an alcohol fugue,
dispensing final judgments with that magical
touch that withered everything on contact.
Looking into his eyes suggested dreams Kafka
would have written about if he could have fallen
asleep after having one. Instead the walking nightmare
chose never to sleep but to ghost walk through
a desiccated world turning black with rot and decay.
Asking him to identify folks he had been with was
as futile as looking into his eyes for signs of life:
there was nothing there to see and there never would be,
there were no memories, only images that could not be
distinguished one from another. Most people had
flophouses to crash in, he had morgue drawers and
toe tags instead of identity bracelets and a cot.
Even the cops wanted no part of arresting him nor
medical professionals, at least not the sane ones, as
what he had was thought to be contagious.
Weaning him from his drugs of choice was unthinkable
given the rages he was prone to.

Every culture has a name for people like him, all of them unspoken. He doesn't so much leave a place as disappear, but where he had been was never the same, nor would it ever be no matter what happens after. What is the half-life of a monstrosity?
The technical term for what was left behind he was responsible for?

The Drunks

I drank to make time stop.
I'm not sure where or when
I learned that. Might have been
when the AA meetings started.
Not that I wanted to go, you know,
like voluntarily. They were court
ordered. Judge said, *You even
want to think about getting a license
again in this state you'll do AA.
Every day. Without fail. For a year.*
So there I was, mildly stoned,
listening to these pathetic losers
tell their boring life stories and all
the while I'm thinking: absolutely
none of this applies to me.
Only problem I have right now is
being sober. Like at this moment.
In this room. With these people.
I thought going to these meetings is
going to require some serious juice
or I am going to go completely crazy.
They just go on and on and on.
Then this woman said that thing
about stopping time and everything
clicked into place: I had an internal clock,
and the more you drank, the less it
mattered what time it was or where you
were. It was clear sailing after that.
No more meetings for me.
Who needs a license, anyway?

Mulholland Drive

The car crash on the avenue that leaves blood and memories
scattered in the grass.

    -Bukowski

The end is the beginning,
there is no changing that now.
All the movies we were cast in
are over, long gone from theaters,
moved to second billing drive ins,
are features the only lovers
left alive, pay no attention to.
Our bodies belong to someone else
now, even as nearly used up as they
are, torn from scripts that should have
had happy endings but never did.
Search and rescue teams find our
remains, once the last vestiges of
life have been squeezed out.
Repurpose them as test crash dummies
up against a laboratory wall.
The scarring that results, makes
what we were, what we imagined
could be, unrecognizable now.
Even our fingerprints and dental
records reveal nothing.
If life was a comedy ours was not
a funny one.
The once lit candle representing
the souls we have lost, is blown out now.
A night owl watches over us but
there is nothing left to see.

Murder by the Numbers

for Marie Colvin

Every morning you see them:
the wives, the mothers,
the sisters and the daughters.

You see them, just before dawn,
on the Path of Death.

Sometimes the snipers shoot.
Sometimes they do not.

When they shoot, they may well
take aim as the women come in,
toward the market, braving death,
to buy food for their families.

Other times, the snipers wait until
all the women have shopped,
then they shoot.

Other times they cannot be bothered.
They are too lazy that morning.
Too tired. Distracted.

It's like a game, sighting the women,
watching them as they come crouched
as low as they can get, moving as fast

as they are able in such an unnatural
position for running. As if making
themselves smaller would change
the outcome once the snipers decided
they will shoot.
Or not.

The snipers have a minute to lead any
woman they choose.
Can let the women create that illusion of:
almost there in their minds and then
Bang, You're Dead.

Fifteen victims down so far and counting.
They never miss.
This is not a made-up story.

Girl on a Bridge

There's always a dark darker than the dark you know.
Hala Alyan, "You're Not a Girl in a Movie"

If she were an all-girl band
they would call her Pussy Riot.
She's a walking, talking, punk rock
gypsy with her bright pink hoodies
bleach stained and bloodied, tied tight
to her cut-by-a-blind-man scissor ruined hair.
Claimed she washed what was left
on her head with kerosene she threatened
to light, dead center, in whatever club
she was appearing in. Changed her eye
color the way other people changed clothes.
Favored lens that seemed to glow in the dark
or ones that made her appear feral, feline,
as wild as a jungle cat that would not stay
in her cage. Sang like a queen of an endless
night, like fingernails raking cracked mirror
glass or a dull razor blade on skin.
Learned that trick where you opened your throat
as wide as it would go and swallowed swords.
Nurtured circus freaks as sidemen and roadies
who taught her the secret of fire breathing.
Warned her never to try that trick inside,
all of them knew that she would, despite knowing
what might happen. Because a warning was temptation.

Because what did happen was inevitable.
Because she could never refuse.
Ah, this was the life!
It was like blood in a double shot glass:
it tasted terrible at first, but after awhile,
you developed a taste for it.

Lessons of Darkness

From Russia with Love

Inside the Exclusion Zone,
this is what the world will look like
after the oligarchs, the kleptocrats,
and demagogues are done raping
the countries, extrapolating their
treasonous desires for more, more, more;
a greed that exceeds all others:

A sheet metal elephant slide in a
now deserted, former playground,
rust flecked and leaf storm buried,
thirty years after radiation leak,
outdoor toy relics encircled by new
growth junk trees, the only ones that
can survive...

All the dust covered plastic toys,
left untended in mid-game by kindergarten
children long gone from here and
everywhere else, pale colors faded
by unfiltered aluminum sun...

Dental charts and medical histories
silver-fished piles of curling paper,
all illegible notes and number now,
referring to nothing...

Abandoned science projects in high school
labs: inactive homemade volcanoes,
broken microscope slides, dissected
frogs shriveled skin and desiccated bones...

Vegetal growth and human decay
co-existing in perfect harmony.

Henry and June

I know the words you long to hear
I know your deepest, secret fear.

> -Jim Morrison, "Spy in the House of Love"

The only poems in her life were
the kind that could be traced on
her skin by lovers. The more bedmates
the better: tall ones, dark ones, insane
ones, who create their own houses
of words like *Black Spring*, crazed riffs
he whispered in her ears as a jazzed up
tone poem, unedited, until it reached
so deep inside her she could only find it
in dreams. Dreams so dark she acted out
on sheets made into a crazy quilt of fabrics
each representing a different, forbidden act:
sleeping with an analyst in transference,
the lost father reclaimed, a bisexual gypsy
guitarist, anyone but the husband who
provided financial support, a man whose
only means of satisfaction was looking
through a peephole into an antechamber,
into a house of seven veils, where his wife
writhed inside, several acts into a psycho
drama that last for years. Three lovers at
one time is never enough.

Movern Callar: "Pray Like Your Mean It"

wife who wore white for another man.
            -Hala Alyan, The Twenty Ninth Year

The way she partied gave new meaning
to the phrase: mood elevators with loud
music. Her face was perpetually aglow
with neon afflicted colors, changing like
computer programmed rainbows, algorithm
infused tricks of light, chemically altered
brains could not assimilate. Her skin
vibrated, were high tension wires in a body
stuck in overdrive pushing currents through
her veins towards terminals where such
massive illusions were not meant to go.
Her personal scent was ozone burning,
rapidly depleting passion, and unstable
elements looking for a place to adhere.

Men on dance floors were an affliction
in bell bottomed trousers, bare chested
bling models, puta focused cruise missiles,
a few coke lines from ignition. Date rape
cocktails didn't faze her: she is nobody's
wife, no one's sex slave, until a final
proposition is made. Even gown dressed for
commitments, the part of her that wears white
was a dancehall wraith on ecstasy, the rest

of her a shell of a body on loan from on-stage
midwives to hunchbacks monsters and hare-lipped
mutants born to dream the dreams others
stay awake for. Felt naked when the veil
was lifted, felt the spotlights focused on who
she was meant to be, who she really was, and
where she was meant to go.

Black and White Night

When he was alive, he was a rock star,
backed up by the dancing girls of death.
Cut songs deep under mottled skin,
leaving marks like pin pricks on the soul.
Went to hell and back in an afternoon,
twice on a weekend night, when the band
was hot and the SRO venues were on fire,
with all the exits locked, and back stage
roadies feeding the flames.
Headbangers fought Black Hell's Angels
over mosh pit bragging rights; the ones
who drew blood first earned a Get Out
of Jail Free card and album covers
of basement tapes made by Satan's Sluts,
the best damn sidemen in a business where
singing lead was everything and doing backups,
or duets, was a dying art.
On tour, in a rented plane, free basing at
ten thousand feet was just another ill-
considered career move.
The short term effect was catastrophic, but
in the long run, had a rock n roll, instant
classic vibe impact; better press than even
the best publicists could provide.
There might not have been a gold record at
the end of the rainbow but where they were
now, who really cared?

Men with Guns

There they are:
the rock stars of revolution:
red berets, jungle fatigues,
criss-crossed rows of ammo,
their chins thrust forward in a
self-conscious, arrogant pose,
proud and fierce, tequila strong
and crystal meth hyped.

These men with guns, locked
and loaded, vague battle plans
discussed, full strike forces armed
and ready for just-before-dawn
raid, for emerging from deep cover,
one surgical strike, one tactical
opposition mission from oblivion.

Their Plan B is non-existent,
appears to be: stand and be delivered,
to become like the Hussein boys:
dead on arrival photo ops for
international TV news hotlines.

No Che Guevaras here, just these men
with guns, destined to be hung like
Benito, by their ankles, upside
down, in public square to be pissed on,
allowed to fester, a public menace/health
crisis in the making.

In two weeks, after they have been cut
down, no one will remember who they were.

Innocents with Dirty Hands

Instead of the jaws of life
they were skilled at applying
the jaws of death. Learned
the rudiments of their art as
youths running skag for street
gangs, doing time in houses of
detention, foster homes, those
places where kids go to learn
necessary skills for the adult life
to come. Even when their juvie
records wiped clean, their reputations
precede them. A Maximum Bob
judge laid out his version of the law:
Hard time in Coxsackie for a nickel
with guaranteed transfer to Big D,
Dannemora, for the second half
of the dime. Or, join the Marines
and let them make men out of you.
What the Marines did for them was
make them stone cold killers well
versed in the art of modern weaponry,
hand to hand, and all the black op
dark arts any man would ever want to
know. Molded them into perfect
killing machines and instilled two
necessary basic components they
did not formerly possess: discipline

and patience. They never had consciences.
and didn't need them.
Saw hell hole combat in deserts, sheer
cliff mountains, and black death jungles,
loving every minute of every mission
they were detailed on. Were so far
off the radar, so far off the books,
no one asked questions about where they
had been or what they did. That they
were still alive and breathing unaided was
all anyone needed to know.
Were headhunted for sick money as
well paid assassins, necessary vital parts
of that ever expanding new growth industry
in the mercenary trade. Thought they had
died and gone to heaven and maybe they
had but were having too much fun to notice.

To Die For

They were Fine Arts majors with music
minors thinking about more practical
matters like switching out music for
Lit. Were children of wealth, beauty
and prosperity, futures assured once
they found the right bloodline to mix
genes with. Never thought they could be
one driving while impaired, substance
abused traffic accident, from oblivion.
Or a legal opiate addiction for pain
management after major plastic surgeries,
facial reconstructions, a doctor's script
could alleviate until it didn't.
Buying Oxy from black market sources
evolved from back room deals to off-campus
crash pads, less and less desirable dealers,
higher prices, as their need increased
and supply dwindled until they replaced
pills with brown cinnamon, Mexicali shooters.
Dropping out of school was a foregone conclusion
and the only bloodline they were concerned with
was the one they stuck drugs in.
First anyone had heard of Fentanyl was
after the, *no you go first tie off* that
resulted in instant OD, no Narcan remedy

could make right. Jonesing for relief,
all the remaining one could do was watch
her friend turn blue, her eyes turn hard as
hand carved ivory dice rolling snake eyes
back into her head with a grim reaper chaser.

Wild at Heart

When he came to the crossroads
of nowhere and somewhere else,
the devil was bestowing gifts:

Second sight to the daughters of Cassandra.
Hot picks for Paganini strings.
Mona Lisa lips to star struck Marilyn twins.

In the moment, he passed up the gifts:

of a singer's perfect pitch,
crazy fingers for jazzman's ivory keys,
the perfect body for the perfect mind.

Settled on what he did best,
to keep on, keepin' on.
The devil smiled and granted his wish
silently adding,...on the dark side of Jesus...
which was where he was headed on his own.
Saw himself as a fallen man made for sinning,
and for wild women, who could really sing
the blues.
Called them all, Baby, and said they were
pretty like a city at night when all you could
see was the artificial night.

Roamed from one sundown to the next,
a tarnished Hohner in his duffel made for
playing in every lowdown bar or garage band jam.
Folks who'd heard him play, swore he could
make that mouth organ talk, make it howl
at a neon colored moon.

Drank pit stop, no label gin, from clear bottles,
hell raised and burned by an invisible flame.
Carried three Morgan dollars in each high hipped
pocket, liked to say, *Where he was going,*
you always need to be ready to pay the piper,
to tip the ferryman on that long, lonesome
river ride, that never ends.

The Ugly American

The story of his life was
a rhapsody upon a theme of
a steel edged blade.
All the beds he slept in were
active crime scenes with all kinds
of forensic evidence.
When he said phrases like:
Felony Indictment, the tone of
his voice suggested he was speaking
of a dream lover.
That when he referenced the word,
predicate, he meant multiple arrests,
as opposed to a part of a sentence,
unless it was used along with trials and
convictions.
Had a cemetery smile: wide open
spaces punctuated by formerly white
capstones.
Drank as if he was accelerating a
personal apocalypse sponsored by
the brewers of Budweiser.
Rubbed the mound that always protruded
from the gap between soiled sweat pants,
and filthy Down and Dirty t-shirt, referring
to his girth as product placement, suggesting
he got paid to be both slovenly and obese.

Add a few tattoos and a loin cloth,
lay him down on a Tracey Emin bed, and
he would have been a one man freak show
as photographed by Diane Arbus, that is if
she hadn't killed herself before getting to
meet him, or maybe she had met him, and
the memory of the meeting was what would
do her in.

Live and Let Die

always a corpse flower, never a bride
        -Emily Skaja

All her co-workers agreed that
she crammed twelve hours of hard
living into six hour shifts she made
seem twice as long than they actually were.
Was born doing sixty in a thirty.
Spent her formative years on the take
while others were playing pickup sticks
and tossing jacks.
Obtained degrees in stimulation and pain
on her back in schools where hard knocks
were invented and honey traps honed to
a fine art.
Graduated with high honors so stoned
on black hash she thought the sky was
was melting in the heat.
Felt like it too
Bartended in biker bars for fun.
Didn't care about the money-it was all
about the excitement of being there.
When asked what she was drinking,
she always said, *Moose Drool.*
Bent down low, tilted her head directly
under the tap, soul kissed the spigot,
and pulled the stick so the brew would go
straight down the chute to where it belonged.

Took her breaks riding bare back in store
rooms where even the shithouse rats wouldn't go.
Had *Candy's* tattooed on her right breast
and *Apples* on the left one.
Didn't care who saw them or where.
Saw more wildass times in one night than
most people saw in a lifetime.
That was what she did on Thursday.
On the weekends, it was the same times ten.
Went on runs with the leaders of the club
just to see where they might end up.
More often than not it was trouble.
The kind of trouble you can't escape from.
Said, *You only live once. Who the hell
would want to do more than that?*
Who Indeed?

Dead Man

Your poetry will be written in blood.
        -Nobody to William Blake

He who talks loud but says nothing. I am nobody.

Riding the train from Cleveland to
uncivilized Western territory like
traveling through uncharted black holes
on an African map. Outside, the passenger,
William Blake Accountant, soon-to-be-
thought-of as a poet sees badlands unfolding,
death images: white skulls of long gone
wild creatures, burning covered wagons,
wigwams, more white skulls.....
Inside the passenger car, fellow travelers
are transformed each time William Blake's gaze
shifts from one reality to another, one harbinger
of doom to the next. What he sees are the same
people, outwardly different but essentially
the same strangers with different outfits, haircuts,
clean shaven or not, single or in pairs.
The coal stoker travels back to from the devil's
work to speak to William Blake, suggests
that you need not worry about going to hell,
you are already there.
Soon, at temporary journey's end, William Blake
will be shot, fatally or not, there is no clear
answer to which it was, and a new journey
begun. One that has so many demons in it,

the way forward will seem like going backward
as if the future is somehow, already past,
that it has no meaning as history. His spirit
guide contends, that, *William Blake you are
a poet. And a painter. And now the killer of
white men.* Only the latter is true.
Regardless of who he is, what he has done
the journey always ends the same way: cast off
in a burning boat by no one, heading nowhere.

Mother Night

The images of herself she cherished
most were the ones of her passing
through walls, through glass, etherous as
as smoke; a smudge of light with skin.
She was always naked then, available
as a flame without a wick.
Images suggested, at time, she might not
have been human, other-worldly, lost
between time zones trying to discover
which dimension she belonged in.
Other times, she dangled, in doorways,
balanced on nothing, held aloft by fingertips
gripping doorsills or from ceilings like
fixtures in search of electrical charge,
of sockets to plug into. Other times,
she blended into tenement walls, adapting
patches of water-stained, floral print paper,
as a disguise hoping the humps on her chest
would not reveal her presence.
Outside, on beaches, she was just another
lump in the sand, a face with closed eyes,
like a conch you could put to your ear and
hear the ocean.
All her life was a negative developing,
under-exposed to minimize the risk of being seen.

Loving her like waking from a dream to discover
you were still asleep; a full frontal assault on
the senses.
When she finally leaves, all that remains
is a vapor trail, soft evidence, like the slime
snails leave as they make their way
through oceans of broken glass.

Throne of Blood

Some saints are untouchable behind glass.
      -Alison Pelegrin

Midnight blue death-head devil worship
masks. Spear pointed staffs for burnt
offering rites at the feet of a concrete christ.
Late, late shows, by-invitation-only, clothing
optional, bonfire dancing. All the pagan
refugees from warring states of mind.
Blood oath pacts and black magic chants
meant to summon the horned one from his
sulfur pits; his strip mines and his minions,
their black lungs on fire. Last rite promenades
down cinder paths, squeaking wheel tumbrel
carts for those too lame to walk, for those
condemned to die. Under the sign of
the hourglass: the gallows noose, three cheers
for the public executioner's axe, the torturer's
apprentice wiles: thumb screws and cranial
clamps liberally applied. Join the queues
for hell with long lines, listen for the carnival
barker's first mate, that made-up man with white
face powder and a lipstick grin who mouths
Black Sabbath sermons, all the sacred words
spoken backwards. All that negative energy
spent attempting to make a blood moon whole
again, to make the world more suitable for
demons, self-possession, witch coven cabals.
All that time wasted, drunk and worse, trying
to prevent the day that always follows night.

Where the Boys Are

For all the Brett Kavanaugh's of the world

They are imprudent creatures for in their present
lover they fail to perceive a future enemy.

"Dangerous Liaisons" as quoted in "The Hand That Feeds You"

The boys, slouched over a bar drinking
dirty martinis talking about girls.
The boys, already high on magic mushrooms,
with their lysergic acid tabs and their parents
unlimited credit cards, bail money safely
tucked away.
The boys, slumming downtown in their, for-
the-night, disposable duds, bought at City Mission
stores.
The boys, discussing which girls to move on,
what the rules of these: encounter and conquer
meetings, will be.
The boys, with their cache of downers and
their date rape agendas, disguised as hail-fellows-
well-met, concealing predator on the prowl instincts.
The boys, and the girls they don't even bother
to seduce, demanding sex, leaving the women not
so much beaten and abused as belittled and defiled.
The boys, after, clothes changed, disguises removed,
freshly showered, comparing notes, cell phone
candid photos, laughing at the sex line
phony numbers they provide for later dates,
discussing the unlovely and the undesirables they
have been with, their private markings, scars.

The boys, with their college degrees assured,
prearranged careers, their mover and shaker futures.
The boys, never bothering to remove texts,
selfies, admissible evidence, never imagining
anything like accountability, of not being
the center of what's happening next.
The boys, and the nightmare lives they have
constructed, slouching over a bar, drinking
dirty martinis.

Elements of Crime

After four years in juvie, he was
voted: Most Likely to Do Hard Time.
Hit the streets like some island of
Dr. Moreau reject mutant, eager to
assert his freedoms, lack of constraints,
in ways that made sense to those who
saw a future for him in Super Max.
Had a world view that was consistent
with those officially designated as
demented and depraved, unbothered by
moral boundaries or empathy.
Blended in with the skate rats and
gutter trash, unkempt and tattooed,
disdainful of anything resembling a
figure of authority. Acquired some
street creds busting heads, scaring
cripples and goofing on the helpless,
all of which seemed the right kind of
stuff to the dropouts of America.
Shagged beers and smokes for all
the under aged scammers as no bodega
counter clerk was about to deny service
to someone who exuded his special kind
of crazy. Made out with all the tramp-
stamped strumpets-in-training who
interpreted his irrational moods as
having an irresistible blend of danger

and cool. Hung loose in dead end projects,
abandoned high rise death traps, where
the serious drop outs lived off the grid,
stealing essentials like electricity, cable TV,
and all the crap food you might care to eat.
Was a one-man Anonymous movement,
an anarchist convention waiting to happen,
waiting for the spark that would energize
the Beast, start the conflagration, a chain
reaction that always had something shaped
like a black mushroom shaped cloud at
wherever the end might be.

Branded to Kill

.....the real world is always waiting for its stars to die.
      -Yukio Mishima

He was born under the sign of
the crooked eye. A man destined
for greatness like a latter day
Richard III with delusions of grandeur
caused by undetected brain bleeds,
hemorrhagic fevers that divided
his brain into islands in a blood stream,
archipelagos with extinct volcanoes
aspiring to a reawakening, for latent
Vesuvius pyrotechnical displays.
All this fomentation bred unhinged
speech, lengthy marathon screeds
that seemed without direction until
clinic tapes were analyzed for content
and form. A strange kind of interior
logic was discovered, a metaphoric
plunge into places previously unknown
none of the lab rat observers knew
how to codify. All they knew was
he had to be confined for the duration
of whatever electrical weather event
he was enduring, strapped down with
sensors detecting every tremor unleashed
inside. After weeks in stir, instruments
recorded an off the chart experience,

a Richer Scale 7 point 5 gran mal
seizure that fissured the reaming cortex
in his brains in ways no one could calculate.
Still strapped down, his body was a deft
shade of lethal white, white as sparking
wires on fresh concrete, his whole bearing
was of a man on a terminal drip his body
refused to recognize.

Pandora's Box

Yellow overhead bar lights shine
just for her, dressed in gypsy rags
scavenged from Costume rental shops,
thrift store drop off boxes, roadside
attraction, going out of business stores.
She's a bad acid trip vision looped on
downers and Long Beach Iced Teas,
playing Patience with Remembrance
cards stolen from funeral home wakes
and vigils she crashes, mourner miming
for tidbits and pickpocket fare,
her body odor and horror movie makeup
giving new meaning to the book title
of her life: *The Air Conditioned Nightmare.*
For the price of a drink she'll tell a fortune,
laying out the face cards on café table
deuces pretending the stolen missives
for the dead were signifiers from the Tarot.
All the news she imparts is bad but
how could it be otherwise living as she was:
one foot in the grave, the other
half way down.

Get Out

There is always a story at the end of a rocket.
　　　　-Marie Colvin

Short circuit street lights,
epileptic, spastic as nightmare
shadowed night. Vestigial trees,
missing limbs, power line amputees,
slow rot blocks of would-be ghosts.

Bad spirit animals. Unleashed,
free range, four legged terrors,
feral as cats, kill or be killed pits,
rabid as squirrels, plague bearing
rats.

Zoned-out-of-existence lots.
Looted display case stores, empty
as Salton Seaside beach fronts;
the deserted and the derelict with
slums attached.

No Exit highways. Double yellow
lines turning red during blood moon
phases.

Hardscrabble loners, mixed species
gangs, half-human, half-something else.

Broke car destination points,
permanent tow away, no parking
curbs.

No signal cell service, call waiting
forever. Hail one of those passing
yellow fever cabs and pray.

Lost Highway

The outfit he was wearing had
blood stains, brain matter, stuff
that couldn't be described on it,
where the cloth wasn't torn and
ragged, as if he'd survived high noon in
the valley of death. As if he had
been part of a reenactment gone
bad. Not a historical reenactment,
like the shoot out at OK Corral, but
a replay of Life, as in existence.
As if it were a reenactment of a process
that involved another existence not
necessarily having to do with this one.
Where he was now.
In a place where it was possible to
experience death by selfie. Not stepping
over the edge of some-Do Not Go
Beyond This Point-edge.
Just an awful death by photograph.
That is, where the essence of life,
the soul, is snatched from inside
the body, on the open market, and
sold for pennies on the dollar.
Or tossed from the open window
of a speeding car along side
of some desert two lane, just for
the hell of it.

Was stumbling along one of those
lost highways as if he was headed
toward a place called Helldarado.
Or else he had just come from there
as if he'd hitch hiked from one state
of existence into another.
As if he'd traded places with an entirely
different person, in another place completely,
so foreign from this one, the contrast was
enough to completely blow his mind.
Found himself in a place where the
other was point man for an Insane
Liberation Front. As if he was in a code red
situation for a top secret operation called
Ice Pick and he was charged with moving
the stalled line along.

He seemed confused, drained of life,
an engine on autopilot burning off
the last fumes of fuel in a leaking tank.
It was like being re-imagined, on Mt. Everest,
waiting in line in the Zone of Death, running
low on oxygen, unable to move up
or down, all the dead ones that came
before and failed, defrosting on newly
exposed cliffs, defrosting in the tightly
focused sun, a few yards from the end.

Bad and Beautiful

All through her peripatetic childhood,
a multitude of cowboy friends of her
mother called her the littlie filly.
Told her some day she would have
her name in lights, would be a star
of stage and screen. Like her mom.
Who saw herself as a rock a billy sweetheart
capable of belting out her own brand of
deep woods soul. But in real life, it was
the fringed halters that made men wild
not her voice.
Made ends meet pole dancing
with back room extras. Was a near-legend
as one of those wild horses that could never
be broke in bed and out. Any child of
hers had to be a bare back baby. *Never cut*
that mane. The told her. *Leave it long*
and silky, though running a comb through it
now and then, wouldn't hurt.
More than a few of them offered to curry
the knots and she let them, playing skin
the cat games with grown men while most
girls her age were skipping rope and chewing
double bubble.
Grew up fast to be the kind
of woman who wore see-through tops,
no bra and pants tighter than second skin.

Had sequined t's that said stuff like:
Black Velvet or Black Beauty, though she
was pale and blonde and never saw the sun.
Had small white crosses on her stare-right-
through-you eyes. Gave all the men who
tried her on for size cat scratch fever,
ate devil dogs in bed, while they lay spent
among the sweat-through sheets, trying to
breathe, dying for a drink. Saw herself as
as Free Love Poster Child, though in real
life she was a Your Mind on Drugs spaced-
cadet-warning to all who would see her.
Made it big, on bill boards, smoother
than velvet, crazy beautiful before graffiti
artists had worked their magic, had sullied
her image from sultry to slut.

Omega Man

He was the kind of photojournalist
who focused on war wounds and
scars.
Took close-ups of the bewildered
and the maimed he collected into
unfinished essays emphasizing his
inspirations: Books of Job and
Revelation.
Critical assessments of his work
accused him of the worst kind of
tragedy tourism, labeled him an energy
vampire who thrived on human misery
and pain.
Said his collected works were a
portfolio of putrescence, pustulent
and repellent.
Observations that amused him
prompting wry comments such as,
*Yea though I walk through
the valley of indelible stains,
I shall revel in all forms of evil....*
Said the dark energy that impelled
him yielded dark matter that may
seem like madness to philistines
but was actually controlled chaos.

Drank Absinthe as if it were the
life blood of some fallen gods,
were the font of inspiration that
led directly to hundreds of rolls
of low resolution film, images that
represented the interior of his mind,
a place so arid all forms of life had
abandoned it following a cataclysmic
event. All the oxygen gone.
The nutrients too.

Altered States

to be haunted is to be dreamt
of in reverse. -Michele Battiste

There was acid in those days,
minds expanding and contracting
like climate change ice floe and
where reflux meant, bad acid
flashbacks. Where the worst kinds
of dreams a person could imagine were
conceived.

Without warning chimerical
face changes, threaten the way
bodies do, crossing over from one
state of existence to another, the way
ghosts do, cross-breeding with the living,
co-existing in a new kind of Dali melting
dream. A place, on an astral plane,
with no fixed landmarks to cling to.
Where visions and worlds collide
and nothing living survives,
nothing rational remains sane.

After the crackup, total breakdown
lane therapies include sense depravation
tanks, immersions, where silence becomes
cacophony, and all the imagined beasts

of the jungle mingle with the real ones,
creating tiny monsters that spread torment
through nerve endings like a blunt force trauma.

New psycho-photo techniques
visualize what lurks within. Create interior
images of mind crafted games of chance,
all the dice loaded, all the high rollers,
figment memories that may never be.
Are all features, dislocated parts, of an imagined
landscape, are the murky images of the places
he'd never been, invisible cities struggling to
be borne. Mornings after these brain baptisms,
these immersions, are spent tethered to
straight backed chairs in full sun morning
rooms, eyes rolled all the way back inside,
inspecting the grounds.

Chinatown

Inside a single-use life, there are no second chances.
-Ocean Vuong

Year of the dragon gangsters, stiletto tough
   and Brylcreme slick
China white nights and mary jane afternoons:
   golden armed and raspy voiced street
   creepers
Sweat shop laundries and steam heated, dry
   pressed, elite shop labels
Snub nose gats and Bunker Hill blasters:
   strong arm demands and protection
   racket scams
Underage flesh merchants, white and yellow
   slave merchants: a pound of flesh equals
   a bowl of O
Shanghai sailors, pocket watch lifters, stab and
   go murder men
Pushcart vendors: "don't ask what's in it" edibles,
   charred dead meat on a stick, buy-it-cheap
   prices
Stolen goods store fronts, you-name-it we've got-it
   more-coming soon-sales: Permits! We don't
   need no stinkin' permits!
Crime family Law and Order strictly enforced:
   step out of line and you pay the ultimate
   price

Mickey Finn House Specialty Cocktails, Bay City
> back alley rollers; strange street music and tin
> pan alley concerts

After the ice cream specials: slumming it debs:
> Don't feed the locals, Don't mingle with
> their trash attitudes, rarely ends well

New Year's Celebrations: Years of the Rat, Dog, Hare.....
> fireworks, gunshots, the whole nine yards;
> the wilder the costume the more the mayhem

Raw sewage in streets of broken dreams, perfume
> valleys and sordid hideaways

White woman in front seat, top down convertible, dead
> shot in broad daylight, just another unsolved
> homicide, just another victimless crime

Chinatown

Girl with the Pearl Earring

Slumming downtown sleaze queen
Single pearl earring and diamond nose stud
Skin tight NYU t-shirt
Second skin designer jeans
Making the Art House scene with clove cigarettes
Carved ivory butt holder
Hopped on white dust carried in antique snuff box
Squirreled away in long strap cloth mini purse
Stair climbing brownstone steps
Third storey loft walkup
Interior decoration by House of Usher
Retro movie posters between floor to ceiling mirrors
Admires Night Porter Nazi vamp Charlotte Rampling when young
Looking as if she would fuck all of the high command
Then skin dive the Dead Sea
Takes refreshment from Jamestown Kool Aid stand
Buys (b)*rats on a stick* from sidewalk vendor
Sees spontaneous Gay Pride demonstration with costumes
Everyone loves a parade onlookers
Like Outtakes from Fellini's *Clowns*
Or *Juliet of The Spirits*
Wonders what movie she is in
Maybe Polanski's *Death and the Maiden*
Maybe Pinter's *Betrayal*
Maybe *Dial M for Murder* the remake

Models nude or clothed
Whatever is necessary she will do it
So many ways to be abused
So many ways to be the abuser
She knows them all
Invents a few of her own
Follows a thin red line home

At Night All Birds Are Black

Even in her forties, she aspired
to bubble bath nude scenes like
the one Sharon Tate bared all for
in *The Fearless Vampire Killers.*
Got the scene and pulled it off.

Saw herself as a silent screen seductress,
a Ligeia of the Electric Hotel,
black widow proprietor in the Overlook
of the Palisades; every room inside
a way station for transports to an
isle of the dead. *Wait for me here,*
she would say to the bewitched,
while I change into something more
appropriate. Something like a shroud,
she must mean, returning, as she does,
made up with white grease paint and
killer angel eyes, weeping blood, and
black death tears, men cannot resist.

They all follow her into the night where
the flocking birds are black and all
the siege balloons are waiting to be
released. At assignations end, all her
consumptive dreams end the same way:

with blood puddles and sleep walks,
over cliffs, sheer gown on fire, a quarter
moon as escort to the water below.

Nights after she is gone, sirens sing
but there is no one left to hear.

Mississippi Burning

Time wasted, spent on dark
Internet web sites, invitation-
only conspiracy/ hate chat rooms.

So much time wasted listening to satellite
radio, Coast to Coast AM/PM 24 hour
hell and damnation talk shows,
money wasted buying end of the world
shelters, arms and ammunition, supplies
and bottled water, never wondering where
the clean water will come from, the power
once the generator dies, the breathable air.

Time wasted researching Nazi Werewolf
Organizations, flat earth societies and harboring
outer space aliens, cave people, American primitives,
all, self educated and feral like High Sierra CHUD's.

Time wasted with like minded,
heavily armed patriot of the new millennium,
whose idea of party hardy was a sky burial
with flaming tiki torches and an executioner's
black hood for chance encounters of
the unwanted kind.

Time wasted, life wasted, money wasted,
all of it for nothing, for a two buck tin star
lawman badge, illegal weapons, unsanctioned
raids on people of color enclaves doomed to
failure before they began.

Time, inside, wasted, spent joining hands, swearing
blood oaths, fidelity to the one and only
lost cause, one prison riot away from dead.

Mommie Dearest

*I am writing because they told me never to
  begin a sentence with because.*

-Ocean Vuong, On Earth We're Briefly Gorgeous

Because she left me along at the seaside room
        during the thunderstorms on St Croix
        and I was terribly afraid.
Because I was five years old and the policeman who
        found me wanted to know what I was doing out
        in the rain, all alone, at night.
Because I told him I was lost and I was looking for
        my mother who left me all alone.
Because all I remember now was how afraid I was.
Because St Croix in 1953 was a Third World Country.
Because you went there to establish residency for one
        year and when you did, you were eligible for
        an uncontested divorce.
Because during that time you went mad but hadn't made
        the time allotment and you had to stay until
        you made the one year time limit.
Because an uncontested divorce was more important
        than anything else.
Because you wouldn't take me to a doctor when my ears
        ached during that time because you didn't believe
        in doctors.
Because you didn't believe in much of anything and the things
        you did believe in where enough to get you certified
        as crazy.

Because I have had a lifetime of tinnitus in both ears and am
    mostly deaf in one.
Because I would get dizzy and pass out and I was always
    losing my balance.
Because I fell out of tree and landed on my head and needed
    hospital care.
Because I had to wear a white cap of bandages until they
    fell off.
Because I got toxoplasmosis from drinking unpasteurized milk
    that didn't show up until I was in my late twenties and
    when it did, I was told I would be lucky if all I did was
    go blind.
Because this was one of those many gifts that just keep giving.
Because I got a bacterial ulcer around the same time that
    began to show up in my teens
Because it was close to forty years of misery a doctor cured in
    ten days once the cause of the pain was diagnosed.

Because I sat on window ledges in second storey apartment
    that had no glass and often felt faint.
Because you insisted it was nothing.
Because a one armed man chased me along the dock and tried
    to molest me and I only escaped because he could not
    climb a fence that I could.
Because you stared out of a window for hours/days smoking
    Camel shorts, drinking coffee, as if I wasn't in the same
    room with you.
Because when we were home on Long Island you accidently
    injured me with a vacuum cleaner handle and I still have
    the scar.

Because after they certified you, I visited you every weekend
        for a year when you were at Pilgrim State and I have never
        been more scared in my life, before or since.
Because of those visits I can never forget what it was like to be
        seven years old.
Because I can no longer distinguish dreams from memories from
        nightmares of what it was like when I was a child.
Because of this, I must copy a line from "On Earth We're Briefly
        Gorgeous," *I'm not a mother, I am a monster.*
Just
Because

Lessons of Darkness

The television is a retribution machine, where,
if one watches long enough, one dies a thousand deaths.

-Rosalyn Drexler

1-

Before the bombing, aerial view oil fields,
               training films for Apocalypse Now!
Alien-seeming settlements on desert plane
               sandscapes; crude black hell holes
               and open pit lakes of flammable waste.
Somewhere on the rainbow slick, featureless
               buildings: storage tanks, devil's apprentice
               barracks, mess halls and Quonset hut
               out buildings.
Old testament biblical verse narrative voice,
               Ring Cycle Music, Liebestod, Tristan
               und Isolde

2-

There is no remembrance of former
things; neither shall there be any
remembrance of the things that are to
come with those that shall come after.
Ecclesiastes 1:11

After the bombing, all the outbuildings gone.
Pits where the people used to be,

Craters rimmed with melted metal truck parts,
        car parts, jeep parts, people parts.
Crispy critters soldered to steering wheels.
Lumps of fleshy heat fused sand textured like glass.
This is what hell now looks like on a Thursday
        afternoon; only the carrion birds moving.

After the bombing, all the exposed walls smoking,
        and endless flattened landscape of fire;
        Kuwait on fire, all the oil fields burning
        expelling black toxic waste clouds

        3-
Four horsemen of the apocalypse pass me by

Alan Catlin is retired from his unchosen profession as a barman. In his spare time, he has been publishing for parts of six decades in little, minuscule, not so little, literary, and university publication: from the *Wormwood Review* to the *Wisconsin Review* to *Tray Full of Lab Rats*, to *Wordsworth's Socks*, to *The Literary Review* and so forth. His chapbook, Blue Velvet, won the Slipstream Chapbook Contest in 2017. One of his more recent full length books is *Last Man Standing*, from Lummox Press, detailing his life and times walking to the bus stop, busing to work, and, at his former job, continuing an earlier, similarly arranged book, the now out of print, underground classic, *The Schenectady Chainsaw Massacre*. For his sins he is the poetry and review editor of misfitmagazine.net, an online poetry journal.

CPSIA information can be obtained
at www.ICGtesting.com
Printed in the USA
FSHW011556110120
65893FS